OUR 42nd PRESIDENT
BILL CLINTON

OUR 42nd PRESIDENT
BILL CLINTON

by Jack Roberts

SCHOLASTIC INC.
New York Toronto London Auckland Sydney

Photo Credits

Front cover: © Bill Clinton for President Committee. Back cover: *Arkansas Gazette*/SIPA-PRESS.

ISBN 0-590-46572-4

12 11 10 9 8 7 6 5 4 3 2 1   3 4 5 6 7 8/9

Printed in the U.S.A.   40

First Scholastic printing, January 1993

Contents

Acknowledgments vii
1. The Convention 1
2. Young Billy Blythe 4
3. Hot Springs High School 9
4. The Peacemaker 15
5. Georgetown University 19
6. The Draft 22
7. Hillary Rodham 25
8. Courtship and Marriage 30
9. The Boy Governor 36
10. Defeat and Reelection 40
11. Tragedy in the Governor's Mansion 44
12. The Education Governor 47
13. The Campaign Begins 51
14. Overcoming Obstacles 55
15. Hillary Clinton: Both Wife and Partner 59
16. Family Man First 63
17. The Issues 67
18. The Baby Boomers 70
19. The 42nd President 75
Chronology 81

Acknowledgments

I wish to thank the following people for their help and generosity:

Nancy Ward, Bill Clinton for President Campaign Headquarters; Dee Dee Myers, Press Secretary; Max Parker, Press Department, Clinton for President; Cara Kelley, Greer Margolis Mitchell Grunwold & Associates, Media Adviser and Public Relations; Elvira Crocker, National Education Association/ Communications; Jean Enochs, American Legion Boys State, Indianapolis, Indiana; and Nancy Kelley and the many friends of Bill Clinton who shared their recollections. Also, special thanks to Linda Bloodworth-Thomason for her film, *A Place Called Hope*.

*We need a new approach to government . . .
based not simply on what each of us can
take, but on what all of us must give
to make America work again.*

— President Bill Clinton

OUR 42nd PRESIDENT
BILL CLINTON

1
The Convention

$\mathbf{A}$ booming voice rang out through the convention hall at Madison Square Garden in New York City at precisely 10:54 P.M. on Wednesday, July 15, 1992.

"Madam Secretary," the delegate called out. But before he could continue, the convention hall erupted with cheering and applause.

"Madam Secretary," the delegate called out again, trying even harder to get the attention of the secretary of the Democratic National Committee. But, still, the noise of the enthusiastic crowd drowned him out.

Nearly 5,000 delegates and thousands of members of the press had packed themselves into the convention hall that night in anticipation of just this moment. And, now, the delegate from Ohio — the man who was about to cast the deciding votes at this important convention — could not be heard.

Finally, as the crowd quieted down, the delegate from Ohio called out for the third time.

"Madam Secretary," he said, "the great state of Ohio — the state that gave us flight and the state that gave us John Glenn — Ohio wants change; America wants change. Ohio casts 144 votes for the next president of the United States, William J. Clinton."

With those votes, forty-five-year-old William Jefferson Clinton captured enough votes to officially make him the Democratic party's 1992 candidate for president of the United States.

Once again, the convention hall erupted. As the band jubilantly played "The Stars and Stripes Forever," confetti streamed down from the rafters while "Clinton for President" banners waved in the air.

As the deciding votes were cast, Governor Clinton stood together with his wife, Hillary, their daughter, Chelsea, and dozens of staff members. They had gathered at Macy's — the world's largest department store, which was only a few blocks from the convention center — to watch the momentous occasion on a big-screen TV.

Soon, Bill and his family would leave the store for the short walk to Madison Square Garden. But for just a moment, Governor Clinton must have thought back over the previous nine grueling months.

It had been a tough campaign. Even before the

first primary election in New Hampshire, there had been questions about Bill Clinton's experience (or lack of experience, some said). He was governor of Arkansas, a poor state with fewer people than the city of Chicago. "Does that give him enough experience to be president?" people asked.

There had also been questions about his character. Did he really dodge the draft during the Vietnam War? Could he really be trusted?

But Bill Clinton hadn't given up. He persevered — just like his grandfather had taught him. And slowly, more and more people started to listen to his ideas. More and more people came to believe that Bill Clinton really was the best choice for the Democratic party and the country.

Now it was time to make his way to the convention center, where he would greet the thousands of delegates who had made it all possible. He turned and hugged his wife as they prepared to leave the department store for the short walk to the convention center. "It's been a long trip," he seemed to say to his wife. "But we made it."

It had been a long trip. Some say it started in the city of Little Rock, Arkansas, on October 3, 1991, the day Bill announced his candidacy for president.

But, others — particularly those who know him well — say his race for the presidency started many years earlier in a little town called Hope.

2
Young Billy Blythe

On August 19, 1946, a young woman named Virginia Blythe gave birth to her first child, a baby boy, in the small town of Hope, Arkansas. She named her young son William Jefferson Blythe IV, after her husband, Bill Blythe.

At the time, Virginia Blythe could not have imagined that her son would grow up to be president. But he did. William Jefferson Blythe IV became William J. Clinton, the forty-second president of the United States.

Young Billy Blythe never had a chance to get to know his father. That's because Bill Blythe was killed in an automobile accident only a few months before his son was born.

The accident happened in Missouri. Bill Blythe, who was a traveling salesman, was driving home from Chicago to Hope when a tire on his car blew out. Bill was thrown from his car and landed face-down in a ditch full of water. He was knocked unconscious and he drowned. He was only twenty-nine years old at the time.

As a result of that tragic event, Virginia realized that she would have to raise her young son on her own. "When you lose your husband," she says, "you never think you are going to get married again. And I didn't feel I was going to be able to earn enough money to support my child."

So, soon after her baby was born, she made an important decision. She decided to leave her son with her parents — his grandparents — so that she could go to college in Louisiana, where she would study to become a nurse.

It must have been a very painful decision for the young mother to make. But, as Bill explained years later, "She endured her pain because she knew her sacrifice was the only way she could support me and give me a better life."

So, for the first four years of his life, Billy Blythe was raised by his grandparents, Eldridge and Edith Cassidy. Some say they were "dirt poor." And, in fact, the old, two-story house they lived in didn't even have a bathroom inside. But, as one relative pointed out about Bill's family, "They were a little more fortunate than the rest of us, because we didn't even have electricity."

Despite those conditions, Bill says he never felt poor. "If you had clothes on your back and a place to sleep and food to eat, and if you had people to love you and to discipline you, you were by definition not poor; you were rich, because you had the elements of a successful life," he says.

During those early years, while his mother was away at college, Bill's grandparents taught the young boy many things. First, they taught him about the importance of education. Even though his grandfather hadn't gone beyond grade school, both he and Bill's grandmother knew how important a good education was.

So, from the time Billy was very young, his grandparents read to him and taught him how to read. They also taught him his numbers and how to count and to add and subtract. Bill can still remember his grandfather telling him over and over again, "You have to learn these things, so you can do better than I've done."

During those early years, his grandparents also taught young Billy about equality. In those days, Arkansas was a segregated state. Yet, Billy's grandfather firmly believed that all people were created equal. And he taught his young grandson to respect all people. "I learned from him to look up to people other folks looked down on," Bill has said.

By working hard, Eldridge Cassidy saved enough money to open a small grocery store in Hope. When people from the neighborhood would come into the store without any money, he would let them buy groceries on credit. "There were no food stamps back then," Bill says, "so when his customers — whether white or black — who worked hard and did the best they could came in with no money, he'd give them food anyway." It was a lesson in kindness and helping others less fortunate.

Bill learned one other thing from his grandfather. As Bill explains it, his grandfather ". . . taught [me] to live with my failures and disappointments and get up again and again and again."

In other words, Eldridge Cassidy taught his grandson persistence. He taught him to stick with a job until it was done, no matter how difficult it was or what obstacles came up.

Billy Blythe learned his lesson well. Even as a young boy, his mother recalls, Bill always finished whatever he started, even if it was "building a little sand castle or whatever."

That lesson was an important one. Years later, when he was running for governor, and then even later when he was running for president, Bill would face many difficulties. He would also face many serious obstacles in his career. And there must have been times when Bill thought he might not be able to overcome those obstacles.

But each time a new obstacle appeared, Bill would simply struggle that much harder to overcome it. He would persevere. He learned about perseverence from his grandfather.

When Billy was four years old, his mother returned to Hope and married an automobile salesman named Roger Clinton. A few years later, Roger moved the family north from Hope to Hot Springs, Arkansas.

After moving to Hot Springs, Bill's mother became concerned about the quality of education her son would get in the Arkansas public schools. That's because for years the public schools in Arkansas were considered by many people to be the worst in the nation, bar none. So Virginia enrolled her son at St. John's, a private Catholic school.

By the time he was in third or fourth grade, Billy Blythe had become known as Billy Clinton. But Bill didn't legally change his name to Clinton until he was fifteen years old.

When Bill was ten years old, his mother gave birth to a second child, Bill's half brother, Roger, Jr.

A year later, Bill's grandfather Eldridge died. Bill was eleven years old. It must have been a terribly sad time for young Billy, who loved his grandfather very much. "He was the kindest person I ever knew," Bill says.

Bill would live in Hot Springs until it was time to go to college. But it would be the little town of Hope — where he spent the first seven years of his life — that he would always remember as his home. It was in Hope where he learned the important lessons that would guide him the rest of his life. Thinking back on those important years, Bill says simply, "All I am or ever will be came from there."

3
Hot Springs High School

"**H**i, how are you? My name's Bill Clinton, and I'm running for president."

The year was 1962, and Bill Clinton wasn't running for president of the United States; he was running for president of his junior class.

His candidacy that year didn't come as a surprise to any of his classmates. From the time Bill Clinton entered Hot Springs High School in 1960, he always seemed to be running for one class office or another. In fact, he ran for so many different offices that he earned the nickname "Billy Vote Clinton."

Years later, when Bill announced he actually was going to run for president of the United States, his former high school friends didn't find that surprising, either. "Even back when we were in high school," says Glenda Cooper, a former classmate, "we always thought, well, someday Bill will be president."

Carolyn Staley, one of Bill Clinton's oldest friends, agrees. She says that in high school, whenever she saw anything with a picture of the White House on it or anything that was "presidential" looking, she immediately thought of Bill.

"Billy Vote Clinton" won the election that year for junior class president. But the following spring he won something that would change his life. He was selected to attend the American Legion Boys State in Little Rock.

Boys State and Girls State are leadership programs that are designed to help young people learn more about how government operates. The young people become "citizens" of a model state and then participate in electing public officials, including state senators.

In order to attend Boys State, young men must meet certain requirements. One of them simply states that a boy must have completed his junior year in high school.

But another requirement states that "only boys with outstanding qualities of leadership, character, scholarship, loyalty, and service to their schools should be considered for Boys State." As a high school student, Bill Clinton was clearly such a boy.

One of the highlights of the Boys State event is the election of two senators. This is an important election because the senators then get to attend Boys Nation in Washington, D.C.

In 1963, Bill was one of the young men elected senator from his Boys State in Little Rock. So that summer Bill made his first trip to the nation's capital. There he met many public officials, including one of the real senators from Arkansas at that time, Senator J. William Fulbright.

Senator Fulbright had always been somewhat of a role model or father figure for Bill. After the meeting, the two stayed in touch, and a few years later Senator Fulbright gave Bill a part-time job that made it possible for Bill to stay in college when he was running short of money.

Bill also got to meet the man who was president of the United States at that time, President John F. Kennedy. The President came out to the White House Rose Garden to greet the senators from Boys Nation. There, young Bill Clinton shook hands with President Kennedy and had his picture taken with him.

"I remember thinking," says Bill, "what an incredible country this was that somebody like me, who came from a little town in Arkansas, who had no money, who had no political position or anything else, would be given the opportunity to meet the president."

When he returned home, Bill gave his mother the picture of himself with John Kennedy. As he handed the picture to her, Virginia says she knew at that very moment that her son was going to go into politics as a career. "I could just read the expression on his face," she says. After that, she never had any question about what he was going to do in life.

Throughout both elementary school and junior high school, Bill had been a very good student. But at Hot Springs High School, he excelled. He got excellent grades in every subject.

In addition to being a good student, he was also a popular young man with many friends. Many of those friends thought he looked a little like the rock-and-roll singer Elvis Presley. So Bill would entertain his friends by doing impersonations of Elvis, singing "Blue Suede Shoes" or "You Ain't Nothing But a Hound Dog," two of Elvis Presley's early hits. Even today, some of his staff still jokingly call him Elvis.

Although he didn't participate in organized school sports very much, Bill loved basketball. Friends remember that he wasn't very coordinated, though. Years later, during his campaign for president, he got into a pick-up game one day. During the game he took eleven shots, but made only four. And, according to reports, he forgot to dribble most of the time.

But even though he may not have been a star athlete, he was a star musician. He even thought for a while about becoming a professional musician after he graduated.

Bill played the tenor sax. And he was good. As his band director remembers, "He could sight-read with the best."

Every summer, Bill attended band camp in Fayetteville. One year, he won first place in the state band's saxophone section. He also played with a high school jazz group.

Bill was so good with the sax that he could have won a music scholarship to college. But he decided against it, for one reason. Even though he was good at the sax, he felt he would never be great. And he knew he could be great at something.

Like many other teenagers in the early 1960s, Bill and his friends often listened to famous folk singers, such as Peter, Paul, and Mary. One song they were sure to have listened to time and time again was called "If I Had a Hammer." It was a song about justice and equality for all people. "If I had a hammer," the group sang, "I'd hammer out justice . . . I'd hammer out a love between my brothers and my sisters, all over this land."

Young Bill believed in those words. He had grown up believing in equal rights for all people.

In the early 1960s, a black Baptist minister named Dr. Martin Luther King, Jr., was becoming famous for his nonviolent struggle for racial equality. In 1963, Dr. King gave a stirring speech at the Lincoln Memorial in Washington, D.C. The speech became known as the "I Have a Dream" speech. In part, Dr. King said, "I have a dream that my four little children will one day live in a nation where they will not be judged by the color of their skin, but by the content of their character."

Bill had grown up believing in equal rights for all people. And when he heard this speech, he was so moved by it that he memorized the whole thing. Today, Bill still considers it to be the greatest political speech of his lifetime.

"I remember where I was when Martin Luther King gave that speech," Bill says. "I was home in Hot Springs all by myself. I just wept like a baby all the way through it."

According to Bill's half brother, Roger, religion and church-going were always important to Bill as he was growing up. "He loved singing the hymns and gospel music," Roger says, "and to this day it's still an important part of his life."

Bill graduated from Hot Springs High School in 1964. He ranked fourth academically out of a class of more than 300 students.

Throughout his youth, Bill was considered to be a "model son." He never seemed to get into any trouble. Once, a friend of his said, only half-jokingly, "Don't you *ever* do anything wrong? You're a teenager . . . you're supposed to do things wrong."

There was a reason why Bill worked hard at being a good boy — a good son. But no one — not his closest friends, not his teachers, not even his pastor — knew what that reason was. That's because no one knew the terrible secret Billy Clinton was hiding.

4
The Peacemaker

Young Bill Clinton was an excellent student, a popular friend, and a model son. But he also hid a terrible secret. It was a secret that caused the young boy enormous pain. It was a secret that forced him to grow up fast. And it was a secret that taught him special skills as a "peacemaker."

Bill's secret was that his stepfather, Roger, was an alcoholic. Usually, his stepfather was an easygoing, loving man. But when Roger drank, he became violent. Often he would beat his wife and Bill's younger brother, Roger.

Bill's feelings as a young boy must have been similar to those of many young children who live with alcoholic parents. Often, the children blame themselves for the fighting. In many cases, they believe they can stop the arguing and the violence simply by being a "good" boy or girl.

For many years, Bill kept this part of his life

very private. He didn't tell anyone about the terrible trouble at home.

Today, Bill says, "I didn't know I was supposed to talk about it. I was raised in that sort of culture where you put on a happy face, and you didn't reveal your pain and agony."

Even Rose Crane, a good friend who lived in a house directly behind Bill's, didn't know that Bill's father was an alcoholic. "Bill and I ate supper at each other's house; we played together most afternoons, but I didn't know Roger Clinton was an alcoholic," Rose says. In fact, she says that most people in Hot Springs didn't know that Roger was an alcoholic until it came out in the newspapers during Bill's presidential campaign.

Over the years, Bill worked hard at keeping his parents from arguing and fighting. As a result, he learned special ways to keep peace in the family. He learned how to break up a fight between his parents and to "smooth over the violent quarrels at home." He learned how to be peacemaker.

But no matter how good or successful Bill was in school, no matter how hard he tried to keep peace in the family, the drinking and the violence at home didn't stop. His stepfather would go on binges when he would drink heavily. His mother would then throw her husband out of the house for a period of time. Then she would take him back. And the trouble would start all over again.

By the time Bill was fourteen years old, he was taller and bigger than his stepfather. One night, young Bill finally decided that the family had taken all of the abuse they would take.

As his mother remembers, young Bill came into the room where his stepfather was sitting. Bill asked his stepfather to stand up, telling him he had something he wanted to say to him.

Roger had been drinking, and was a little slow in getting up, Virginia remembers. So Bill said, "Daddy, if you're not able to stand up, I'll help you; but you must stand up to hear what I have to say."

Finally, Roger stood up. Then, Bill looked him straight in the eye and very quietly and calmly said, "You will never hit either my mother or little brother again. If you want them, you'll have to go through me first."

His stepfather didn't quit drinking, but from that moment on, the fighting and the violence and the physical abuse stopped.

Nevertheless, his parents continued to argue. Finally, when Bill was fifteen years old, his mother decided to get a divorce. In her petition for a divorce, she told the court that her husband had ". . . continually tried to do bodily harm to myself and my son . . ."

The divorce was granted. But, three months later, the couple was remarried. Roger had promised he would change, and Virginia felt that Roger, Jr., needed a father.

It was at about that same time that Bill decided to change his name to Clinton legally. He told his friends that he wanted to change his name so that both he and his younger brother would have the same last name.

But many people believe that Bill had another reason for changing his name. They say that by changing it, he probably felt it would help to bring his family closer together. It was yet another example, they say, of how Bill always tried to be a peacemaker.

Looking back, Bill says that his childhood was very difficult. "I was raised to believe that no matter how tough it gets for you, there are always a whole lot of people worse off. I struggle now to reveal my true feelings. . . . It's a real hard thing for me to do. . . ."

He also doesn't like to talk too much about his childhood. During Bill's campaign for the Democratic nomination for president, his speech writers would try to include some lines about his difficult childhood, but Bill would take them out. "C'mon," he'd say, "that sounds too self-pitying."

Thinking back on those years, Bill says that he now knows that his stepfather really did love him. "I came to realize that he was a good person and the problem was not that he didn't love me and my mother or my brother," he says. "The problem was that he didn't think enough of himself."

Eventually, Bill made peace with his stepfather. But that would not happen until Bill's senior year at Georgetown University in Washington, D.C.

5
Georgetown University

If someone offered you a part-time job for $3,500 a year, or a full-time job for $5,000 a year, which would you take? When Bill Clinton was faced with such a choice, it didn't take him long to answer. "I'll take *two* part-time jobs," he said.

The job was working for Arkansas Senator J. William Fulbright. The year was 1966, and Bill Clinton had just started his junior year at Georgetown University.

If it hadn't been for that job, Bill might not have been able to finish college at Georgetown. He had enrolled there in the fall of 1964 but, by the summer between his sophomore and junior years, he was out of money. The job on Senator Fulbright's staff helped make it possible for him to continue his studies there.

Bill had won a scholarship to Louisiana State University. But from the time he was a junior in high school, he knew he wanted to study politics.

So he went to his guidance counselor to ask her to recommend schools that offered a good program in international affairs. The only one she could think of at that moment was Georgetown University in Washington, D.C.

The fact that the school was in the nation's capital was enough to convince Bill that Georgetown was the college he wanted to attend.

Almost as soon as he arrived at Georgetown, Bill became a popular student. He was elected president of his class in both his freshman and sophomore years.

During his years at Georgetown, former high school classmates and friends often came to visit him. Carolyn Staley was visiting when Dr. Martin Luther King, Jr. was killed. After the assassination, riots broke out in Washington, D.C., as well as in other parts of the country.

Today Bill says that, like many people, he was heartbroken when Martin Luther King, Jr. died. "It broke the hearts and spirits of millions of people," he says.

Both Bill and Carolyn wanted to help. So they jumped into his old white Buick convertible and volunteered to deliver groceries to the areas where the rioting was going on.

During his senior year, Bill's professors encouraged him to apply for a Rhodes scholarship. Each year, this scholarship is given to a very special group of students so that they can go to graduate school at Oxford University in England.

The scholarship program was established in 1902 by Cecil John Rhodes. In his will, Rhodes said that he did not want "merely bookworms" to receive the scholarships. Rather, he wanted the scholarships to be given to young men who showed certain qualities. Those qualities were "truth, courage, devotion to duty, sympathy for and protection of the weak, kindliness, unselfishness, and fellowship."

Bill Clinton was clearly such a young man. Yet, at first, Bill didn't want to apply. He didn't think he stood much of a chance of winning this prestigious scholarship. But he did win the award, and today Bill Clinton is the only president of the United States who has ever won a Rhodes scholarship.

In the fall of 1968, Clinton would board the S.S. *United States* to sail to England and go to school at Oxford. Two years later, he would enter Yale University Law School in New Haven, Connecticut. Before enrolling in Yale, however, Bill would face an agonizing decision.

6
The Draft

When Bill Clinton boarded the S.S *United States* in October, 1968, to sail to school in England, his country was in turmoil.

Martin Luther King, Jr., the great civil rights leader, had been assassinated in Memphis, Tennessee, earlier that spring.

Senator Robert Kennedy, brother of former President John F. Kennedy, had been assassinated only two months later while campaigning in Los Angeles for the Democratic nomination for president.

And an unpopular war in Vietnam, a little-known country in Southeast Asia, was claiming thousands of American lives.

Like many young men and women in the 1960s, Bill opposed the war in Vietnam. But he also felt he had a duty to serve his country. That fall at Oxford, he and his friends spent hours upon hours debating the war and talking about their uncertain future.

Then, during the winter of his first year at Oxford, Bill received a letter from his draft board. The letter told him he was classified 1-A. That meant he was eligible to be inducted into the Army. The letter also told him, however, that he would be allowed to finish his term at Oxford.

Bill was then faced with a difficult decision. He could either be inducted into the Army, or join an officer training program at an American university. Since Bill had planned to go to law school, anyway, he finally decided to join the army ROTC (Reserve Officer Training Corps) program at the University of Arkansas Law School.

In the fall of 1969, however, Bill changed his mind and returned to Oxford. At the same time, he notified his draft board of his decision. That meant he was no longer deferred.

In a letter to a friend at that time, Bill said he had changed his mind because he felt he was "running away." He added, "Everyone else's children seem to be in the military, most of them in Vietnam." Bill must have felt he also had a duty to serve.

That fall, however, President Richard Nixon began a new system for selecting young men for the Army. The new system involved a lottery. Every day of the year was randomly assigned a number from 1 to 365.

A person whose birthday happened to be assigned a lower number would most likely be drafted into the Army. A person whose birthday was assigned a higher number would most likely not be called up for military service. Bill's birth date was assigned number 311. That meant there was little chance he would be inducted.

Soon after the lottery was held, Bill applied to Yale University Law School, where he was accepted for the fall 1970 term. At the same time, he wrote a letter to his ROTC commander at the University of Arkansas. In it, he said, in part, "I want to thank you . . . for saving me from the draft. . . ."

Years later, during his campaign for president, that letter would become public and some people would accuse Bill Clinton of being a draft dodger because of it.

7
Hillary Rodham

In 1961, a young girl named Hillary Rodham made an important decision about her life. She decided she would become an astronaut.

So the young teenager wrote to the National Aeronautics and Space Administration (NASA) to ask what she should do to become an astronaut. NASA wrote back and told her they were sorry, but they weren't accepting girls in the astronaut program.

The teenager was infuriated. Why, she wondered, shouldn't a girl have just as much right to be an astronaut as a boy?

It would take another seventeen years before NASA would accept women into the astronaut corps on January 16, 1978, and another five years after that before Sally Ride would become the first American woman in space.

By then, Hillary Rodham, the young girl who wanted to be an astronaut, would be a successful lawyer. She would also be a professor of law at the University of Arkansas in Fayetteville, Arkansas, and she would be the wife of an up-and-coming young politician named Bill Clinton.

Hillary Rodham was born in Chicago in October 1947. Four years later, her family moved to Park Ridge, Illinois, a middle-class suburb of Chicago near O'Hare Airport. Her father, Hugh Rodham, was a salesman in Chicago and, later, the owner of a small textile business. Her mother, Dorothy, was a housewife.

Hillary was the oldest of three children. She had two younger brothers: Hugh, who was two years younger, and Tony, eight years younger.

From the time she was very young, Hillary was taught to stand up for herself and speak her mind. "I was determined that no daughter of mine was going to have to go through the agony of being afraid to say what she had on her mind," her mother says.

By all accounts, Hillary was a popular girl. As she recalls, she "earned every Girl Scout badge," and one year she was elected president of her high school class.

One of the most important people in her life during that time was her Methodist youth minister, the Reverend Don Jones. He taught her and other teenagers in the area about equality.

Park Ridge was an all-white community. But

Reverend Jones wanted the young people to know nonwhite kids.

Reverend Jones would take the youth group to visit black and Hispanic teens from the south side of Chicago. Once he even took them to Chicago to hear a speech by a young black minister who later became known throughout the world. After the speech, Hillary and her friends stood in line to shake hands with Dr. Martin Luther King, Jr.

Back then, there were a lot of farms in the area where Hillary grew up. Migrant workers would come to the area to work on the farms. Reverend Jones also set up programs that would get Hillary and her friends involved with baby-sitting for migrant children while their parents worked.

In high school, Hillary was an excellent student. But as she grew older, she saw something that bothered her. Many of her girlfriends, who were smart students, began worrying that boys would ignore them if they appeared to be too smart. So they would often pretend not to know the answers to questions in class, or they would not take certain courses that were considered too difficult for girls. They didn't want to appear smarter than their boyfriends.

Hillary couldn't understand that. "I can recall thinking, 'Gosh, why are they doing that?'" she said years later. "It didn't make sense to me."

After she graduated from high school in 1965, she went to Wellesley College in Wellesley, Massachusetts. When she arrived, she thought of herself as a Republican. But slowly her ideas began to change. And by the time she graduated from Wellesley, she was a Democrat.

Hillary was not as radical as many college students were at that time, but she loved to talk about politics and current events. As one classmate recalls, "She would rather sit around and talk about current events or politics or ideas than go bicycle riding or to a football game."

Hillary, in fact, helped organize the first anti-Vietnam War protest at Wellesley College.

As her graduation approached, a group of students had an idea. There had never been a student speaker at a Wellesley graduation ceremony. Many students thought it would be a good idea, and they asked Hillary to be the pioneer.

In her commencement speech, she talked about what it was like to be a young adult during the second half of the 1960s. During this time, the United States had become more and more involved in the Vietnam War, Dr. Martin Luther King, Jr., and Robert Kennedy had both been assassinated, and there had been race riots in many American cities

"You and I must be free not to save the world in a glorious crusade," she said, "but to practice with all the skill of our being the art of making possible."

The speech gave Hillary her first taste of national publicity when it appeared in both *Time* and *Life* magazines.

After graduating from Wellesley in 1969, she entered Yale University Law School. That was where she first met another young Democrat who would eventually become her husband. His name was Bill Clinton.

8
Courtship and Marriage

Bill Clinton first saw Hillary Rodham in a class they were both taking at Yale University Law School. It was almost love at first sight. "I knew from the minute I saw her," he says, "that if I got involved with her, I would fall in love with her."

But he was afraid to speak to the attractive young brunette. So for the next few weeks he simply stared at her every chance he got.

One day they were both in the law school library. "I'd been trying to work up the guts to speak to her," he says. But, again, all he could do was stare.

Finally, the young woman walked across the room and over to Bill. "Listen," she said, "if you're going to keep staring at me and I'm going to keep staring back, we should at least know each other's name. My name is Hillary Rodham. What's yours?"

Bill Clinton was so shocked that this young woman had actually come over and spoken to him that he became very flustered. And at that very moment, he could not remember his own name.

Thinking back on that day, Bill says that he was terribly embarrassed. "But," he adds, "we've been together, more or less, ever since."

Bill Clinton had entered Yale University Law School in New Haven, Connecticut, in the fall of 1970. He had won a scholarship to study at Yale, but it didn't provide enough money to cover all of his expenses. So, he took a variety of part-time jobs. Sometimes he held as many as three part-time jobs at once.

As soon as he met Hillary Rodham, the two began dating and spending a great deal of time together. But as things got more serious, Bill faced a dilemma. Hillary was an outstanding student, and he knew that she could have a great career as a lawyer in New York City or Washington, D.C.

But he also knew that he didn't want to go to a huge city after he graduated. He simply wanted to return home to Arkansas and perhaps become a small-town lawyer.

Bill was falling in love with Hillary. But he didn't think he could expect her to give up her career to move to a poor little southern state like Arkansas.

So, after they graduated in 1973, the two separated. Hillary went to Cambridge, Massachusetts, to work for the Children's Defense Fund. Six months later, she moved to Washington, D.C., to work on a committee that was looking into the possible impeachment of President Richard Nixon.

Bill got into his car and headed home to Arkansas. Before he left Yale, he had heard about a job teaching at the University of Arkansas Law School, in Fayetteville. So on his way home, he called the dean of the law school to talk about the job. At first, the dean told him he was too young for the job. But, true to his nature, Bill persisted. And he got the job.

Even though Bill and Hillary were now living in different places, they continued to carry on a long-distance romance. They often talked on the phone about their careers, about politics, and about their lives apart.

From the moment Hillary met Bill, she liked him. "I thought he was great looking and he was fun and he was somebody who challenged you and made you happy all the time. I had never met anybody like Bill," she says. So it must have been difficult for her to be many miles away from the man she was falling in love with.

Later that year, Hillary made her first visit to Arkansas to see Bill. He picked her up at the airport in Little Rock, and then drove her to his mother's house in Hot Springs. Usually, the trip takes an hour. But that day, it took more than eight hours.

Bill was so proud of his home state that he wanted to show Hillary everything. And he did. He took her all over town, stopping at his favorite places — from state parks to fast-food restaurants. Undoubtedly he boasted about the fact that Arkansas — and the town of Hope, in particular — grows the biggest watermelons in the world. Some grow as big as two hundred pounds.

Hillary returned to her job in Washington, and the long-distance romance continued. Then, in August 1974, President Richard Nixon resigned from office. That meant that Hillary's job on the impeachment committee had come to an end. At the same time, Bill Clinton was making his first bid for Congress.

Earlier that year, Bill had decided to run for the U.S. Congress against the Republican incumbent, Representative John Paul Hammerschmidt. At the time, the people in that part of Arkansas were staunch Republicans. So, few people thought that this young, unknown Democrat had any chance of winning at all. But he proved them wrong.

The bid for Congress was the first time that Bill entered a political race, and one of only two times in his career that he ever lost. And even though he lost that year, it was a close race. He received 48 percent of the vote.

During the campaign, Hillary decided to go to Fayetteville to help Bill. After all, she had been traveling back and forth between Washington and Fayetteville for some time in order to visit Bill. She had also begun to like the small but charming town.

Then, while she was working on the campaign, she got an offer to teach at the University of Arkansas Law School, where Bill was also teaching. Suddenly, she was faced with a difficult choice. She could return to Washington, D.C., where she was certain to have an outstanding career of her own in politics, or she could stay in Fayetteville with the man she loved.

She decided to take some time, visit some friends back East, and hopefully sort things out in her mind and decide what she really wanted to do. Bill took her to the airport and, on their way, they passed a house that was for sale. Hillary casually mentioned that she liked the house.

When she returned from her trip, Bill picked her up. They drove to the house she'd mentioned that she liked. "Well, I've bought it," Bill said. "So now you're going to have to marry me."

Hillary, however, had already made up her own mind. As she puts it, her heart won out.

Although Bill had lost the election for Congress that year, he had won Hillary's heart. In October of 1975, the two were married. During the reception, Bill told the guests that he planned to seek elected office again in 1976. He wasn't sure whether he would run for Congress or try for some other public office. But one thing was certain: Bill Clinton would be running again.

Sure enough, in 1976, Bill ran for Arkansas State Attorney General. Bill had made many friends throughout the state during his campaign for Congress two years earlier. Those friends now helped him win the position of Attorney General.

That meant he and Hillary would have to move to the state capital in Little Rock. It also meant that Bill Clinton was one giant step closer to the governor's mansion.

9
The Boy Governor

Imagine what it would be like to be the youngest governor of any state in the country.

Bill Clinton knows exactly what it is like. On January 10, 1979, at the age of thirty-two, Bill was sworn in as governor of Arkansas.

That made him not only the youngest governor in the nation, but also the youngest governor of any state in forty years. The only governor who was younger than Bill when he took office was Governor Harold Stassen of Minnesota — and he was younger by only a few months.

As soon as he took office, people began calling Bill the "boy governor." They frequently asked him how it felt to be the youngest governor in the nation. His answer was always the same: "I plan to concentrate on being the best governor rather than the youngest," he said.

When Bill entered the race for governor in 1978,

there were four other candidates. All four were older than Bill.

But Bill had something they didn't have. Some call it "charisma" — a special quality that makes a person especially attractive and interesting to other people. Bill was good-looking, he had a unique ability to get his ideas and messages across to others, and he was smart. As one person said, ". . . he had an intellect that rivaled any other ever seen in the service of the state."

Only four short years had passed from Bill's first political race in 1974 to his election as governor of Arkansas in 1978. Both Bill and Hillary were almost stunned by how quickly things had happened. A good friend of theirs at the time remembers their first night in the governor's mansion. "We were kind of roaming around this giant mansion. We were eating chocolate chip cookies and sort of saying, 'Are we really all here?' "

Bill's future as a politician seemed bright. In fact, not too long after he took office as governor, there were rumors that he might be chosen as President Jimmy Carter's vice-presidential running mate in 1980. There was only one problem.

Even if Bill had been chosen to run on the Democratic ticket that year, he couldn't have accepted. That's because the United States Constitution says that a candidate for vice-president must be at least thirty-five years old. At the time of the election in 1980, Bill would have been only thirty-four.

Then, suddenly, things began to fall apart. First, the Arkansans didn't like the fact that his wife,

Hillary, continued to use her maiden name, Rodham. They seemed to want a traditional first lady who would take her husband's last name, rather than a feminist who would keep her own last name.

People also felt that Bill had become far too interested in national politics, and therefore wasn't paying close enough attention to the problems of Arkansas.

At the same time, people began to believe that being governor had "gone to his head." One magazine said at the time that Bill gave the impression of being an "arrogant whiz kid who had surrounded himself with a bunch of outsiders who looked on Arkansans as barefoot hicks."

Another writer got right to the point when he reported that the people simply didn't like Bill's "highfalutin' ambitions." They said he "put on airs."

But the straw that broke the camel's back was that he raised the fees for registering a new car and for getting an automobile license. Even though the tax was to be used to improve the highways, most people in Arkansas were outraged. So, as his first two-year term in office was coming to an end, the people of Arkansas decided to teach their "boy governor" a lesson.

Bill had been nominated by the Democratic party for reelection. His Republican opponent was Frank White.

Throughout the campaign, the polls showed that Bill was ahead. But on election night, something surprising happened. White won by 32,000 votes out of a total of 840,000 votes that were cast. Suddenly, the youngest governor in the nation became the youngest ex-governor in the nation.

Many people — even those who voted against him — were surprised that he lost. "We only wanted to teach him a lesson, not defeat him," one voter explained.

Looking back on that first term as governor, Bill says he understands why he was defeated. "I simply didn't communicate to the people that I genuinely cared about them. . . . I think maybe I have the appearance of trying to do too many things and not involving the people as I should. . . ."

In January 1981, Bill, Hillary, and their ten-month-old baby, Chelsea, stood before the Arkansas legislature to say good-bye. For most people it seemed like the end of the line for this young politician. They figured he was washed up in politics. They said he would never hold public office again.

But Bill Clinton knew that one day he would prove them wrong.

10
Defeat and Reelection

For almost a year after he was defeated for a second term as governor in 1980, Bill stayed out of public life. During that time, he traveled throughout the state. He talked to thousands of people, asking each of them what he had done wrong and what he could do better.

What he found out was that he simply had come on too strong. He had tried to do too much too soon. He also discovered that the Arkansans didn't like the fact that he had brought in so many outside advisers — people who they felt didn't really know Arkansas or its people.

But what they told him in a nutshell was that he had simply gotten too big for his britches.

Bill listened and he learned. And by the end of the first year of Frank White's term, people began talking about a comeback for this young politician.

In January 1982, Bill made a television commercial in which he apologized to the people of Arkansas. He told them he ". . . felt remorse for the errors that were his responsibility while in office and that he wished again for the opportunity to serve." He said that he felt he had made a mistake by not making himself more available to the people. He vowed to reform.

Soon after that, Bill announced his candidacy for reelection.

Once again, Bill's Republican opponent was Frank White. It was a tough but fair campaign. And when election day rolled around, Bill was voted back into office for a second two-year term. An amazing 72 percent of the registered voters turned out, giving Bill 55 percent of the vote. This was the beginning of what would become the longest tenure by one person in the Arkansas governor's mansion. Bill Clinton was, once again, a "young, bright political star."

The reason for his success the second time around was clear. He had learned his lesson well. "I learned the hard way that you really have to have priorities and make them clear to people. You have to win people over. And to do that, you have to spend some time listening to them."

Even Hillary had listened and learned. On the day that Clinton announced his candidacy for reelection, Hillary changed her name to Clinton. She explained her decision by saying that, in the end, it was more important to the people that she have his name than it was to her to use her own.

Bill's success the second time around may also

have been because he was older and more mature. "He was no longer the young person out to change the world," said one Arkansas official. He made changes more slowly, and was more practical in his approach. And he was more careful about choosing issues to support.

Education was one of those issues. "Over the long run," he said during his 1983 inaugural speech, "education is the key to our economic revival and our perennial quest for prosperity." It was a theme he would return to time and time again throughout his political career.

In 1984, Bill ran for a third term as governor. Once again his Republican opponent was Frank White. During that campaign, White learned just how tough a competitor Bill Clinton really is. As White acknowledged years later, "You can hit him with everything you've got, but you can't knock him out."

With the election of 1986, the term of office for governor of Arkansas changed from two years to four years. Bill ran for his fourth term in office and was easily reelected.

At that time, he told the people, "I would be astonished if I ran again. I think ten years as governor is a long time. . . . I don't want to get burned out, and there are other things I should be doing with my life."

By the middle of 1987, Bill was thinking about running for president in 1988. But one July afternoon, something happened that changed his mind.

Bill was at the governor's mansion when his

young daughter, Chelsea, then only seven years old, came into his office to see him. "Daddy," she said, "Mom says we might not go on vacation because you might run for president."

Bill told his daughter that it was true. He was thinking about running for president. So Chelsea replied, "Well, if you do run for president, we'll just have to go on vacation alone."

Some say it was at that moment that Bill decided not to run for president in 1988. He knew how difficult a campaign for president would be. He also knew how much time it would take — time he wanted to be able to spend with his young daughter. And he knew that, as in many political campaigns, Chelsea would hear negative things about him that would be difficult for her to understand. So he decided not to make a bid for president — at least, not that year. But the seed had been planted.

In 1990, Bill won his fifth term (and his second four-year term) as governor, receiving 57 percent of the vote. During that campaign, he had promised the voters that he would not run for president in 1992. But he would soon ask the people of Arkansas to let him out of that promise.

11
Tragedy in the Governor's Mansion

In 1984, Bill came face-to-face with the toughest decision he would ever have to make. But it wasn't a political decision; it was a personal one. It was a decision that would put his younger brother in jail for dealing drugs.

The heartbreaking ordeal began one evening when the head of the Arkansas State Police came to see Bill. The police commander told the Governor that he had some bad news. "I hate to tell you this, Governor," the officer said that night, "but one of our informants is buying drugs from your brother."

The police commander went on to tell Bill that they did not believe that Roger was a serious drug dealer. "He's an addict," the officer said, "and sells drugs mainly to support his drug addiction."

Bill was stunned. How could he not have known

this about a brother he loved so very much? he asked himself.

The police commander then told Bill they could do one of two things. They could arrest his brother immediately. But rather than do that, they wanted to set up a "sting" operation. That meant undercover agents would continue to buy drugs from his brother over a period of time. Then, when they finally did arrest Roger, they would have a better chance of finding out from him who his suppliers were.

Bill immediately agreed to go along with the "sting." Then he waited. Six weeks went by before the police arrested his brother. It was the most difficult six-week period of Bill's life.

During that time, he agonized over whether or not his brother or even his mother would ever forgive him. But, as he told U.S. News & World Report years later, "I had to be governor — not brother, not son."

At the same time, Bill and Hillary read everything they could about drug abuse. They wanted to understand what might have caused his brother to turn to drugs. And they wanted to know how they might be able to help him.

Finally, the arrest occurred. Roger was convicted of dealing drugs and served a one-year prison term.

At first, Roger was extremely angry at his brother. Later, he realized that Bill had actually saved his life. Today, Roger says that he had become an alcoholic at an early age, and then moved on to drugs.

During this terrible ordeal, Bill, his mother, and his brother went to family counseling. As a result of those sessions, Bill says that he learned a great deal about himself. He learned how his own ambition had blinded him to the needs of his family.

Since his arrest and conviction, Roger has recovered and now works as a television production assistant in California. His admiration and love for his brother are boundless.

When Roger was growing up, his brother, Bill, was his best friend. "He was my brother. He was my father. He was my protector," Roger explains. As adults, Bill was again his brother's protector.

12
The Education Governor

Suppose a sixteen-year-old friend of yours told you one day that she was thinking about dropping out of school. What would you tell her?

You might talk to her about how difficult it is to get a job without a high school diploma. Or you might point out that all her friends would be in school during the day, so there would be no one to hang around with.

If you lived in Arkansas, you might add one other thing. You could tell her that if she drops out of school, her driver's license would be taken away.

That's because there's a law in Arkansas that says if students drop out of school before they are eighteen, their driver's license will be revoked. That was just one of the education laws that Bill Clinton helped pass while he was governor.

The quality of education has been a big concern

of Bill's ever since he was a young boy. One day, in fact, when Bill was about seven years old, he came home from school with some disturbing news. He had read somewhere that Arkansas public schools were the worst in the nation.

"You know," he said to his mother that day, "if Arkansas will let me, one of these days I'm gonna get us off the bottom."

Thinking back on that day, his mother says, "Well, you don't pay a lot of attention to a child saying something like that."

Years later, as governor of Arkansas, Bill did do something about it. On the day he was sworn in as governor for his first term, Bill said, "For as long as I can remember, I have believed passionately in the cause of equal opportunity, and I will do what I can to advance it."

And so he did. Over the next few years, he set limits on how large classes could be; he made parents pay a fifty-dollar fine if they missed a parent–teacher conference; he raised teachers' salaries; and he required both elementary and secondary schools to have a full-time guidance counselor.

There was one new law, however, that caused a great deal of controversy. He made Arkansas the first state requiring teachers to pass a basic skills exam to continue to teach. Out of 32,000 teachers in the state, only 1,400 (fewer than 5 percent) either failed the test the first year the new law went into effect, or refused to take the test and quit.

At first, many people — including many teachers — disagreed with his ideas about how to improve education. For example, some thought that making parents pay a fine for not attending a parent–teacher conference was wrong.

But Bill disagreed. "I believe that anything society does to strengthen family responsibilities and give schools the chance to teach is acceptable," he told his critics. Since parents are an important part of a child's education, he added, "I don't see anything at all wrong in fining them for failing to do their part."

But the biggest outcry over Bill's new education laws came from teachers about the basic skills test. "It seemed to be an injustice," says Viola Moore, a fifth- and sixth-grade teacher from the Mississippi River delta. She had taught for twenty years and felt that it was wrong to now have to prove she was competent to teach.

"But when we calmed down, we saw . . . it didn't really hurt us," she adds.

Slowly, people began to see improvements in the public education system in Arkansas. When Bill first became governor in 1979, barely 36 percent of all high school students in the state went on to college. Today, that number has risen to 52 percent, which is about the average for all states in the U.S. In addition, Arkansas now has the lowest dropout rate in the south. But, as Bill laments, "We still have one student in every four drop out."

During his campaign for president, Bill made a number of suggestions for how the country might help improve the education of all young people. One of his suggestions was that each state be graded every year just like students are.

"I think there ought to be a report card in every state, every year, on the progress of every school and district toward meeting the national education goals," he said.

When George Bush was elected president in 1988, he said he was going to be "the education president." But many people felt he didn't live up to that promise.

So when Bill announced his candidacy for president in Little Rock on October 3, 1991, he promised to be "the real education president." Many people were thrilled to hear his pledge. But there were still many other issues he would have to address. And his campaign was just beginning.

13
The Campaign Begins

Can a little-known governor from a poor southern state become president of the United States? When Bill Clinton announced his candidacy for president, few people thought the answer was yes.

Governor Bill Clinton proved them wrong, of course. But it was a long, hard battle from the governor's mansion in Little Rock, Arkansas, to the White House in Washington, D.C.

That battle for the presidency began on October 3, 1991. On that day, Governor Clinton announced he would seek the Democratic nomination.

Most people at that time said that Bill's chances of winning the nomination — let alone the national election — weren't very good. There were many reasons.

First, hardly anyone outside of Arkansas had ever heard of Bill Clinton. If anything, they remembered him for a speech he gave at the Democratic National Convention in 1988. The speech was so long and boring that the only time he received applause was when he uttered the words, "And in conclusion . . ."

Second, even if he won the nomination, he would then have to face George Bush, the Republican incumbent. Only once in the last thirty years had a Democratic candidate beaten a Republican incumbent. That was in 1976, when Democrat Jimmy Carter defeated the Republican incumbent, Gerald R. Ford.

Finally, if that weren't enough, there was also one other simple fact: Throughout the history of our country, there had never been a president from the state of Arkansas.

In other words, Bill Clinton didn't stand a chance, people said. Case closed.

But what those people didn't know was that Bill Clinton grew up with persistence and determination.

The first Democratic primary election was held in New Hamsphire on February 18, 1992. At that time, five other Democrats had announced their candidacy: Nebraska Senator Bob Kerry, former Massachusetts Senator Paul Tsongas, Iowa Senator Tom Harkin, former governor of California Jerry Brown, and Virginia Governor Doug Wilder.

Bill Clinton came in second to Paul Tsongas in that election. But his second-place finish didn't faze Bill. He called it a victory, and dubbed himself "the comeback kid." Case reopened.

Over the next few months, Bill went on to win the Democratic primary in every big state in the country, including New York, Illinois, California, Florida, Ohio, and Texas.

In April 1992, three months before the Democratic National Convention, *Time* magazine took an opinion poll of the American people. Only 39 percent of the population thought Bill Clinton was honest and trustworthy enough to be president.

Bill believed the people felt that way simply because they didn't know him. So he worked even harder at getting out to meet the voters. He went on television talk shows and traveled around the country, meeting people and talking with them.

Soon after he was officially nominated by the Democratic party, *Time* magazine took another public opinion poll. This time, 58 percent of the people said they believed that Bill Clinton was honest and trustworthy enough to be president. (By contrast, in the same poll, only 59 percent of the people said they thought that then-President Bush was honest and trustworthy enough to be president.)

By July 1992, when the Democratic National Convention was held in New York City, only two candidates remained in the running: former governor Brown and Governor Clinton. By then, however, Bill had won enough primaries to insure his nomination at the convention.

But he had paid a big price to gain the nomination. Almost from the beginning, there had been some serious accusations that almost brought his campaign to an end.

In order to win the election, he knew he had to face those obstacles head on.

14
Overcoming Obstacles

"**W**hen you are running for the presidency . . . and the public has to judge whether you can defend the national security," Bill told a news reporter early in the campaign, "they want to see how you deal with trouble, how you handle yourself when things blow up."

During Bill's campaign, the people had many opportunities to see how this young candidate would handle tough situations. That's because throughout the campaign, there were serious attacks on his character. There were charges of draft-dodging, questionable ethics, and infidelity.

But through it all, Bill held fast. And he proved that when things do "blow up," he can handle them.

The trouble began almost as soon as he announced his candidacy for president.

First, there were accusations that he had had an affair with a singer. Bill flatly denied that charge, saying the "story is just not true."

But he did admit that his marriage had been "less than perfect." At the same time, he insisted that he and his wife, Hillary, had worked things out and intended to be together "for the next thirty or forty years, whether I run for president or not."

Hillary agreed. "My marriage is solid," she said, "full of love and friendship."

Next came a question about the use of marijuana. Had he ever smoked marijuana? the press asked time and time again. Finally, Bill told the press that he had tried it one or two times when he was going to school in England, but that he didn't inhale.

Many people didn't understand his answer. How could someone "try" marijuana, but not inhale? they asked.

Bill's mother, Virginia, provided the answer. On a television news program just before the convention, she explained: "Ever since Bill was little he has been allergic to smoke," she said, adding that even when she used to burn leaves when he was a kid, he had to leave because of the smoke.

A third incident that caused many people a great deal of concern occurred at the end of March. Bill had taken a couple of days off to relax from the campaign. One day during this brief vacation, he played golf at a private country club in Little Rock. It was an all-white club that did not allow blacks or other minorities to be members.

Many people were outraged that he would play golf at a segregated club. And Bill quickly admitted that he had made a mistake. He also vowed never to play at that club again until it was integrated.

Perhaps the most damaging charge that came out during the campaign, however, was that Bill Clinton was a "draft dodger."

It's true that Bill never served in the military. But, as he pointed out, he had personally made himself eligible for the draft and was classified 1-A. That meant he was physically fit for military service.

The charge that he was a draft dodger must have troubled Bill very much. One day during the campaign, a young teenager told Bill that his father had fought in the Vietnam War. The teenager then added that he didn't think Bill was fit to be president since Bill hadn't fought in the war.

Bill must have felt very hurt by this remark. But he looked the teenager directly in the eye and answered him with honesty and compassion: "I deeply respect what your father did, and I applaud it. But you don't know what you're talking about and you can't know because you weren't there, and I hope you never have to learn."

By summer of 1992, many people still questioned whether or not Bill Clinton had the honesty and the integrity to be president.

These attacks on Bill Clinton's character had been very painful. But through it all, he managed to survive and continue on. And through it all, he demonstrated strength of character.

As one person saw it, Bill Clinton "managed to survive a personal ordeal unlike any other in the history of presidential campaigning, and showed more than his share of grace under pressure in the process."

15
Hillary Clinton:
Both Wife and Partner

"**J**ust because I'm the wife of the president," said Sarah Polk, wife of the eleventh president of the United States, "doesn't mean I'm going to be content to simply keep house and make butter. . . ."

The year was 1845, and Sarah Polk's bold statement surprised and angered many people. Yet, true to her word, Sarah Polk went on to become an important and influential voice in her husband's administration.

Nearly 150 years later, Hillary Clinton made a similar remark that also shocked and angered many people. During the campaign, she was asked by a reporter why she hadn't resigned from her job in an Arkansas law firm after her husband became governor.

"I suppose I could have stayed home and baked cookies and had teas," she snapped. "But what I decided to do was fulfill my profession, which I entered before my husband was in public life."

Her critics attacked her for her remark. "She seems to think you are less worthy as a person if you stay home and take care of the kids," one woman fumed. "It's elitist," others sniffed. "There's nothing wrong with a woman wanting to stay at home and take care of the family."

Hillary immediately regretted making that statement. That's because, as she told the press later, she strongly believes that being a mother and a homemaker is one of the most important jobs any woman could hold. "I honor the women who choose to stay home and raise a family," she said. "Those are the choices my own mother made."

Soon after that remark, everyone was talking about "The Hillary Problem." Does she help or hurt Bill Clinton's campaign for president? people asked.

Her supporters said she was an enormous asset to Bill's campaign. They pointed out that Hillary was tough-minded and a good role model for young women.

Other people disagreed. They called her a "pushy feminist" and said she was power-hungry.

They also accused her of dominating her husband, which, they added, was unfortunate. Even former president Richard Nixon said during Bill's campaign that year that a strong wife "makes the husband look like a wimp."

Hillary stood up to her critics admirably. "I think the people value the way I've tried to be a full partner in my marriage and in Bill's life and still be true to my own interests," she told the press.

She must have been right. By April 1992, 55 percent of the people in one public opinion poll said that Hillary was an asset to her husband's campaign. At the same time, 65 percent said they had an overall favorable impression of Hillary, while only 16 percent had an unfavorable opinion of her. By the time the Democratic National Convention was held in New York City, many people were wearing buttons that read HILLARY CLINTON: ONE SMART COOKIE.

And it's true. Hillary Clinton *is* a tough-minded career woman. Twice she's been voted one of the one hundred most influential lawyers in America by the *National Law Journal*, once in 1988 and again in 1991. And, according to her husband, while he was governor of Arkansas, Hillary played a major role in everything he was able to accomplish.

There is another side of Hillary — the side that insists on spending as much time at home with their daughter, Chelsea, as she spends on the road campaigning. "Hillary is very family-oriented," says her mother, Dorothy Rodham.

Hillary admits, though, that she wasn't prepared for the harsh things many people said about her during the campaign.

One day, just before her husband was officially nominated for president, Hillary was asked how she felt about the long and difficult campaign. In response, she simply recited this nursery rhyme: "As I was standing in the street as quiet as can be . . . a great big ugly man came up and tied his horse to me."

Today, President Clinton praises his wife for her many outstanding qualities. She is "far better organized, more in control, more intelligent and more eloquent than I am," he says. He also said during the campaign that if he were elected president, he would consider Hillary his partner as much as his wife.

Sarah Polk died just before her eighty-eighth birthday in 1891. She had lived long enough to see the beginning of equality for women, and she greatly approved of the new roles that women were starting to take on.

"It is beautiful to see how women are supporting themselves," Sarah said shortly before she died, "and how those who go forward independently in various callings are respected and admired for their energy and industry."

Sarah Polk would have liked Hillary Clinton.

16
Family Man First

What kind of man is Bill Clinton really? It's a question that people ask his friends all the time. And there are many different answers. One answer is that he is a man with a great sense of humor.

"I love to crack jokes; I love to laugh; and I don't mind making fun of myself," Bill says. To prove it, he occasionally does an impression of Elvis Presley.

For relaxation, Bill likes to play golf or read, particularly mystery novels. He also likes to jog, or play a card game called Hearts, and play the saxophone. He even played the sax on a TV talk show during his campaign for president.

If Bill had to pick just one favorite leisure-time activity, however, it would probably be doing crossword puzzles. He's been doing them for years. Even as a young boy, he and his best friend would race to see who would be first to finish the puzzle in the newspaper.

Bill says he loves all kinds of music, from gospel to country to pop. But he's particularly fond of Ray Charles. "I think he's wonderful," he says. But no one would be surprised if Paul McCartney, Michael Bolton, or Judy Collins were to entertain at the White House. They're also some of Bill's favorite singers.

There's another answer, however, to the question "what kind of man is Bill Clinton really?" That is: He's a family man — a loving husband and a great dad.

In February 1980, Hillary gave birth to the couple's only child. They named their baby daughter Chelsea, after a Judy Collins version of the song "Chelsea Morning."

Today, Bill says that the birth of their daughter was the most incredible and important experience of his life.

His wife agrees, adding that Bill is a wonderful father. "He's not only loving and supportive," she says, "he's also interested in Chelsea's life and views."

When Bill decided to run for president, Chelsea was eleven years old and a seventh grader at a public school in Little Rock. Bill sat down to talk with her about his interest in running for president. He wanted to see what she thought about the idea and wanted to warn her that a presidential race would be tough. "They'll say terrible things about me," he told his young daughter that day.

Chelsea responded with wisdom and humor. "Dad," she said, "they already say terrible things about you. You ought to go to my school. You can't imagine the things they say. You just got to blow it off and go on."

Like most young girls her age, Chelsea enjoys all sorts of activities. Just before the Democratic convention in July 1992, for example, she attended a summer camp in Minnesota. There, she studied a foreign language. Later that same summer she went to a ballet camp.

In her spare time, Chelsea likes to play softball, even though she confesses that her dad will sometimes embarrass her when she plays by jumping up and down and waving his hands. "But," she adds, "that's okay."

Her parents have always believed that children have certain rights. So when Chelsea was eight years old, they let her decide which church she wanted to join: her mother's church, the First United Methodist Church, or her father's church, Immanuel Baptist. She chose her mother's.

Except for only two years of her life, Chelsea has lived in either the governor's mansion in Arkansas, or the White House in the nation's capital. Yet, her parents have worked hard to protect her from the press and all the publicity that surrounds the family.

"Children deserve to have some childhood and some innocence," Hillary maintains.

When she grows up, Chelsea says she would like to be an astronautical engineer and go into space to build space stations and colonies. It's the same dream Chelsea's mother had as a young girl but could never fulfill.

When asked what she would like the American people to know about her parents, Chelsea thinks for a moment and then says: "I would like America to know that they're great people and they're great parents. They taught me that I had to think for myself and they taught me to treat other people how you would want to be treated and to follow the Golden Rule."

Perhaps Chelsea's answer is the best indication of all of what kind of person Bill Clinton really is.

17
The Issues

The Democratic Convention was still a week away; the national election was four months away. Yet, many people had already decided who they would vote for on Election Day, November 3, 1992.

Some, like thirty-one-year-old James David, from Spokane, Washington, were 100 percent for Bill Clinton. When asked why he was in favor of Clinton, David echoed the opinion of many people with this comment about the Governor. "He's had a lot of fastballs thrown at him," David said. "And he could have given up. But he didn't. He kept on fighting because he obviously believes in himself and his ideas."

Other people, however, had a different opinion. California resident Richard Powell, for example, said he didn't think Clinton had done very much to help the state of Arkansas. "I don't see Arkansas as being any shining example of a state that we should be wanting to imitate," Powell said. "Their economy and their pollution — what kind of record is that? I don't trust professional politicians anymore."

Still other voters were undecided as they weighed the issues that Bill had talked about throughout his campaign.

They thought about his support for what he called the "deadbeat dad" law. That law would force fathers to pay child support.

They thought about his belief that all young Americans should have college loans available to them, but only if they pay back the money either "as a small percentage of their income over time, or with a couple of years of national service as teachers, police officers, child care workers," or similar jobs.

They thought about his position on welfare. He would offer welfare to able-bodied people for no more than two years, and only if they agreed to receive training in parenting and job skills during that time.

And they thought about his promise to all Americans about health care. "In the first year of a Clinton administration," he said, "we'll deliver quality, affordable health care to all Americans."

In a television interview shortly before the convention, Bill was asked what he thought were the five core principles that defined what his goals would be as president. Without hesitating, he listed them:

1. The government is not working; we are going to have to change both parties.

2. We have to put people first. That means we have to put education and training above everything else.

3. We have to have an economic program that will help this economy grow.

4. We have to get control of health care costs and make affordable health care available to everyone.

5. We must come together across racial and ethnic lines.

"The 80s were about 'every man for himself,'" Bill concluded. "The 90s are about 'we're all in this together.'"

Throughout his campaign, Bill talked about these issues to the people. But as the convention approached, there was still one last question people had: Who would Bill Clinton choose to be his vice-presidential running mate? On July 9, 1992, in Little Rock, Arkansas, Governor Clinton announced his decision.

18
The Baby Boomers

The call came at exactly 11:15 P.M. on Wednesday, July 8, 1992, one week before Governor Bill Clinton would officially be nominated by the Democratic party for president of the United States.

"You'd be an excellent president," Bill said to Tennessee Senator Al Gore that night, "and, if you're willing, I'd like you to be my running mate in the election."

There was a brief pause. Then Bill turned to the others in the room, who were anxiously waiting to hear the Senator's answer, and gave a thumbs-up. Senator Gore had accepted Bill's invitation to be his running mate on the Democratic ticket.

The next day, everyone was talking about the "baby boomer" ticket. The phrase "baby boomers" refers to the generation of people who were born in the years following World War II.

When they were nominated by the Democratic

party, Bill was forty-five years old and Al was forty-four. That made them the youngest team ever to run for president and vice-president of the United States.

Many people were thrilled to hear that Bill had chosen Al Gore as his running mate. Al is "tough and smart," said Michael Dukakis, former Democratic presidential nominee. Then he added, "He'll chew up Vice-President Quayle."

But others didn't agree. They attacked the young baby boomer team, saying they were too young and inexperienced to be in the White House. Senator Jake Garn of Utah, for example, called them "pretty boys" and said they had ". . . spent their entire waking moments since they were teenagers planning and plotting their political careers."

To a certain extent, that was true. Al Gore's father even admitted that from the time his son was born, Al was "raised for politics."

Senator Gore was born on March 31, 1948, in Carthage, Tennessee (population 2,500), a short drive from Nashville. His father, Albert Gore, Sr., was a congressman and senator from Tennessee. Al's mother, Pauline, was a lawyer.

As a young boy, Al attended St. Albans Episcopal School for Boys, a private prep school in Washington, D.C. There, he was a good student and enjoyed playing basketball and football.

After high school, Al went to Harvard University in Cambridge, Massachusetts, and graduated in 1969. Throughout his college career, he dated a young woman named Mary Elizabeth ("Tipper")

Aitcheson. The two had met at his high school senior prom, and in 1970 they were married.

The wedding must have been a joyous occasion. Yet, at the same time, Al was facing a serious decision in his life. He had to decide whether or not to join the armed forces. Like many young people, he strongly opposed the war in Vietnam. Yet, he also felt he had an obligation to his country.

So, finally, he decided to enlist in the Army, and in 1970 he was inducted. Soon afterward, he was sent to Vietnam where he served for six months.

In 1971, Al was discharged from the Army and went home to work as a newspaper reporter in Carthage. But politics was in his blood. So in 1976 he ran for Congress and won. Eight years later, he was elected to the Senate, where he became one of the Senate's leading authorities on the environment.

In 1987, Tipper Gore, who has a master's degree in psychology, almost became more famous than her husband. That year, she began a campaign to have record companies put labels on certain record albums, tapes, and CDs. She wanted to alert consumers to recordings that had bad language and songs about sex, drugs, or violence.

Many people accused her of being in favor of government censorship. But she said people had a right to know what they were buying.

In April 1989, a tragic event deeply affected the Gore family. The family had gone to an Orioles baseball game at Baltimore's Memorial Stadium.

After the game, when they were leaving, Al's young son Albert suddenly pulled away from his father's hand and ran into the traffic. The young boy was hit by a car and almost died. It took months for the young Al to recover.

For a long time, Al felt extremely guilty about the accident. He felt he should have been watching his young son more closely. At the same time, Tipper was very angry about the accident.

It was an emotionally stressful time. So Al and Tipper and their family underwent psychological counseling to help them deal with their feelings about the accident. Today, Al recommends counseling for anyone who is going through a difficult time. "I strongly recommend to any family undergoing an experience remotely similar to what we went through not to be afraid to do this," he told the press during the campaign.

Looking back on this tragedy, Al says, "It was a shattering experience for our whole family. And yet it has been in so many ways a great blessing for us. I never thought at the time I'd ever be able to say that. It completely changed my outlook on life."

At the Democratic Convention in 1992, millions of people got to meet the Gore children for the first time, including the three girls — Karenna, then age eighteen; Kristen, fifteen; and Sara, thirteen — and, of course, young Albert, age nine.

In many ways, both Vice-President Al Gore and President Bill Clinton are alike. Both are from the south; both went to excellent schools; both are married to strong women; both are about the same age.

There's also one other similarity: Both have a great sense of humor. In his acceptance speech for vice-president, Al said, "I've been dreaming of this moment since I was a kid growing up in Tennessee; that one day, I'd have the chance to come here to Madison Square Garden and be the warm-up act for Elvis."

The day after Bill made that late-night call to Senator Gore, the two of them talked to the press.

"I come from Carthage, Tennessee," Al Gore began. "I've never been to Hope, Arkansas. But I'm told that Hope is just like Carthage in one respect: It's a place where people know about it when you're born and care about it when you die."

19
The 42nd President

In 1956, ten-year-old Billy Blythe watched the Democratic National Convention nominate Adlai Stevenson for president. It was the first time the young boy had seen a presidential nominating convention on television and he was fascinated. Throughout the convention, he reported the events in detail to his family as they happened.

Thirty-six years later, more than 22 million people watched the grown-up Billy Blythe — now Bill Clinton — stand at the podium of that same national convention to accept his party's nomination for president.

In one of the most powerful speeches of his career, Bill Clinton called for a "New Covenant" between the American people and their government. "We offer our people a new choice based on old values," Clinton told both the delegates at the convention and the millions of people watching at home. "We offer opportunity. And we demand responsibility."

The Democratic National Convention was held in New York City during the week of July 13, 1992. One month later, on August 19, 1992, the Republican National Convention nominated the incumbent President, George Bush, as its presidential candidate. Once again, President Bush selected Vice-President Dan Quayle for his running mate.

For the next seventy-six days, the two leaders — Republican George Bush and Democrat Bill Clinton — battled for the White House. It was a tough fight and a long three months. During those months, Bill talked often about the "New Covenant." The New Covenant, he said, involves hard work, thrift, social responsibilities, and the importance of families, whether they are single-parent families or two-parent families.

Those were the same topics that Bill described in his rousing acceptance speech for the Democratic nomination in New York City. He began that fifty-five-minute speech by talking about his vision for all Americans. Here are excerpts from the speech.

> *Tonight, I want to talk with you about my hope for the future, my faith in the American people, and my vision of the kind of country we can build together. . . .*
>
> *We meet at a special moment in history, you and I. The cold war is over; Soviet*

Communism has collapsed, and our values — freedom, individual rights and free enterprise — have triumphed. . . . Now that we've changed the world, it's time to change America. . . .

I don't have all the answers. But I do know the old ways won't work. . . .

That is why we need a new approach to government . . . I call it a New Covenant, a solemn commitment between the people and their government, based not simply on what each of us can take, but on what all of us must give to make America work again. . . .

What is the vision of our New Covenant? An America with millions of new jobs in dozens of new industries moving confidently into the 21st century. . . . An America in which the doors of college are thrown open once again to the sons and daughters of stenographers and steelworkers. . . . An America in which health care is a right not a privilege. . . . An America in which middle-class families' incomes — not their taxes — are going up. . . . An America with the world's strongest defense, ready and willing to use force, when necessary. An America at the front of the new global effort to preserve and protect our natural environment, and promoting global growth. An America that will never coddle tyrants, from Baghdad to Beijing. An America that champions the cause of freedom and democracy, from Eastern Europe to Southern Africa. . . .

In the end, the New Covenant simply asks us all to be Americans again. Old-fashioned Americans for a new time. Opportunity. Responsibility. Community. When we pull together, America will pull ahead. . . . But I can't do it alone. No President can. We must do it together. . . . I want every person in this hall and every citizen in this land to reach out and join us in a great new adventure to chart a bold new future. . . .

Somewhere at this very moment, [a] child is born in America. Let it be our cause to give that child a happy home, a healthy family, a hopeful future. Let it be our cause to see that child reach the fullest of her God-given abilities. . . . Let it be our cause that when she is able, she gives something back to her children, her community and her country. . . .

Let that be our cause and our commitment and our New Covenant.

It had been a long journey from that little town in Arkansas where Bill was born to the nation's capital. But despite the passing of time, Bill Clinton never forgot where he came from.

"Sometimes late at night on the campaign plane, I look out the window and think how far I am from that little town in Arkansas.

"And yet in many ways I know that all I am or ever will be came from there — a place and time where nobody locked their doors at night, everybody showed up for a parade on Main Street and kids like me could dream of being part of something bigger than themselves.

"I still believe these things are possible; I still believe in the promise of America; and I still believe in a place called Hope."

On January 20, 1993, William Jefferson Clinton — a man from a place called Hope — was sworn in as the forty-second president of the United States.

Chronology

August 19, 1946 — Born William Jefferson Blythe IV in Hope, Arkansas

1953 — Moves to Hot Springs, Arkansas

1961 — Legally changes his name from William Jefferson Blythe IV to William Jefferson Clinton, his stepfather's surname

Summer 1963 — Meets President John F. Kennedy at Boys Nation in Washington, D.C.

Fall 1966 — Works part-time for Senator J. William Fulbright in Washington, D.C.

1968 — Graduates from Georgetown University in Washington, D.C.

1968 — Wins Rhodes scholarship to study at Oxford University in England

1973 — Earns a degree from Yale University Law School

October 1975 — Marries Hillary Rodham in Fayetteville, Arkansas

1976 — Elected Arkansas State Attorney General

January 10, 1979 — Sworn in for first two-year term as governor of Arkansas

February 27, 1980 — Daughter Chelsea is born

January 1983 — Sworn in for his second two-year term as governor of Arkansas

January 1985 — Sworn in for his third two-year term as governor of Arkansas

January 1987 — Sworn in for his first four-year term as governor of Arkansas

January 1991 — Sworn in for his second four-year term as governor of Arkansas

October 3, 1991 — Announces his candidacy for the Democratic nomination for president in Little Rock, Arkansas

February 18, 1992 — Comes in second in the New Hampshire Democratic primary, losing to former Massachusetts Senator Paul Tsongas

July 9, 1992 — Announces selection of Senator Al Gore of Tennessee as vice-presidential running mate

July 15, 1992 — Nominated for president at the Democratic National Convention in New York City

November 3, 1992 — Is elected President-designate of the United States

January 20, 1993 — William Jefferson Clinton is sworn in as the forty-second President of the United States.

SCHOLASTIC BIOGRAPHY

❏ MP44075-6	Bo Jackson: Playing the Games	$2.95
❏ MP42396-7	Christopher Columbus: Admiral of the Ocean Sea	$2.95
❏ MP45243-6	Colin Powell: A Biography	$2.95
❏ MP41836-X	Custer and Crazy Horse: A Story of Two Warriors	$2.95
❏ MP44570-7	The Death of Lincoln: A Picture History of the Assassination	$2.95
❏ MP45225-8	The Fairy Tale Life of Hans Christian Andersen	$2.75
❏ MP42218-9	Frederick Douglass Fights for Freedom	$2.50
❏ MP43628-7	Freedom Train: The Story of Harriet Tubman	$2.95
❏ MP43730-5	George Washington: The Man Who Would Not Be King	$2.75
❏ MP42402-5	Harry Houdini: Master of Magic	$2.50
❏ MP42404-1	Helen Keller	$2.50
❏ MP44652-5	Helen Keller's Teacher	$2.95
❏ MP44230-9	I Have a Dream: The Story of Martin Luther King	$2.75
❏ MP44336-4	Jennifer Capriati	$2.95
❏ MP42395-9	Jesse Jackson: A Biography	$2.75
❏ MP43503-5	Jim Abbott: Against All Odds	$2.75
❏ MP41344-9	John Fitzgerald Kennedy: America's 35th President	$2.50
❏ MP43827-1	The Life and Words of Martin Luther King, Jr.	$2.75
❏ MP41159-4	Lost Star: The Story of Amelia Earhart	$2.75
❏ MP44350-X	Louis Braille: The Boy Who Invented Books for the Blind	$2.75
❏ MP44154-X	Nelson Mandela "No Easy Walk to Freedom"	$2.95
❏ MP44144-2	New Kids in Town: Oral Histories of Immigrant Teens	$2.95
❏ MP42644-3	Our 41st President George Bush	$2.95
❏ MP43481-0	Pocahontas and the Strangers	$2.95
❏ MP41877-7	Ready, Aim, Fire! The Real Life Adventures of Annie Oakley	$2.75
❏ MP43052-1	The Secret Soldier: The Story of Deborah Sampson	$2.75
❏ MP44055-1	Squanto, Friend of the Pilgrims	$2.75
❏ MP42560-9	Stealing Home: The Story of Jackie Robinson	$2.95
❏ MP42660-5	The Story of George Washington Carver	$2.95
❏ MP42403-3	The Story of Thomas Alva Edison	$2.75
❏ MP45605-9	This Is David Robinson	$2.95
❏ MP42904-3	The Wright Brothers at Kitty Hawk	$2.95